EXOTICS

Poems of the Mediterranean and Middle East

*

NIGEL DENNIS

Author of "Cards of Identity,"
"A House in Order," etc.

NEW YORK, N. Y.

THE VANGUARD PRESS, INC.

ACKNOWLEDGMENTS

Most of the poems and translations in this collection have appeared already in *Encounter*, whose permission to reprint is gladly acknowledged.

With regard to the selection from *The Epic of Gilgamesh*, the author's special thanks and gratitude are due to the prose version under the same title by Mrs N. K. Saunders (Penguin Books) on which this poetic rendering was based entirely. The many variations on the theme and the general treatment are, of course, solely the responsibility of the author.

The short poem of Sumer is based on the cuneiform translation in *History Begins at Sumer* by S. N. Kramer (Thames & Hudson).

The author's thanks are due to Mr Alastair Reid and Mr Giorgio Verrechia for their kind assistance.

'O, epic-famed, God-haunted Central Sea!' (Hardy)

CONTENTS

THE EPIC OF GILGAMESH

I

Uncertain traveller, have you never seen
Gilgamesh's city, the city of Uruk?
Traveller, give me your hand and shoe your foot;
I shall take you, Traveller, and you shall see.

Here, Traveller, stands the outer wall;
Put your foot to the stair and climb upon it.
Traveller, walk this wall, walk to and fro:
Do you see the cornice, that shines like copper?
Do you note the bricks, that were baked with fire?
Do you know the foundations must endure for ages;
That their course was fixed by The Seven Sages?

And now look inwards from the outer wall,
Inspect the rampart and the keep, stare
At the entrance to Eanna's temple; ask:
Was ever a threshold so worn to the touch?
Eanna's temple, built for two godheads:
Anu, Lord of the Firmament,
Ishtar, Lady of Love and War.
Now, tell me, Traveller, could any king
But Gilgamesh have built this city:
With the cornice like copper,
With the bricks baked in fire,
With foundations trenched to stand forever,
With Eanna's temple for Anu and Ishtar?

Gilgamesh the King

Gilgamesh was a man, but no man's son.
All the Great Gods, in conference, created him.
Shamash the Sun God endowed him with his beauty,
And the Great Gods made it a flawless beauty.
Adad the Storm God puffed his belly with courage,
And the Great Gods made it a flawless courage.
Flawless beauty and flawless courage,
Are not these two thirds of all,
Are not these two thirds of being?
Yes, but there still remains one third,
The third that sickens, the third that dies,
The mortal third where the Worm hides.
And such was the making
Of Gilgamesh the King:
Two parts divinity,
One part humanity:
Two that might walk the earth always
If the Worm in the One did not cut the days.

The Young King

But what is the Worm to a king of beauty?
What is the Worm to a king of courage?
What is the Worm to a king so young
That he storms Uruk like a lion in glory?
He corrupts the youths that take his fancy,
Rapes the warrior's wife, the noble's daughter;
No virgin goes to her bridegroom's arms
Before Gilgamesh has forced her loins.
And the old men murmur, and the young mutter:
'Is this our king, is this our shepherd?
Where is the wisdom, where the charity?
Where two parts God, where One humanity?'

The Making of Enkidu

Their loud complaints fly up to Heaven,
Fly to the ears of Her That Creates,
The Goddess Aruru; and when she has listened,
She takes in her fingers a scrap of clay,
Wets the clay and starts to mould;
And as she moulds she tells the Gods:
'Gilgamesh the King has need of a rival,
A second self, a bosom companion.
I shall mould him Enkidu, a figure
Into whom he shall look as into a mirror.
The Goddess of Cattle shall mat his hair
And She of the Corn shall make it ripple;
The God of War shall flex his muscles
And he shall wrestle with Gilgamesh.
One furious heart shall fight another,
One angry brother find an angry brother.
They will love and struggle like warrior twins;
They will carry the fight to the hills and plains
And peace will come to Uruk again.'

Enkidu's Upbringing

Down among the beasts she lets Enkidu fall;
He falls out of the night like a shooting star.
Rough-skinned, mat-haired, he is like an animal.
He runs with the deer to the water-hole;
He rubs his flanks against lions and panthers;
His food is grass; where the plough moves
He never goes; and his stench is a beast's.
He is two thirds a beast but one third a man,
For he has fingers, and he has hands.

'Oh, Father, Father!' cries the Trapper,

13

'I have seen a man two thirds a beast!
His hair is matted, he lives on grass,
But with human fingers he unties my snares
And with human hands he fills up my pits.
When I see his face, I faint with terror;
When I watch his fingers, I foresee hunger.'

So the wise Father said to the Trapper:
'Go to Uruk, the City of Gilgamesh,
And say to the king, who is All-Knowing:

"King, give me a whore
From the shrine of Ishtar,
To seduce a brute,
To change his smell,
To make every beast
Fly from his sweat." '

So the son went to Uruk,
And when he told Gilgamesh
That a man two thirds a brute
But bright as a Star of Heaven
Was loosing the game to the four winds
And filling the game-pits with human hands;
Then Gilgamesh the King, All-Knowing,
Said, as the wise old man had said:
'Go to the threshold of Ishtar's shrine,
The threshold worn to the finger's touch;
Call the whore who does duty there
And take her to the water-hole.'

The Whore's Coming

The Father stands by the water-hole,
The old bird with brilliant eyes;
He watches his son come over the plain

14

And cocks his head when he sights the whore.
He cocks his head as she draws near,
Narrows his eyes to watch the deer
Browsing their way to the water-hole;
The lion and panther treading the track,
And Enkidu with his matted hair
Brushing the flanks of his wild brothers.

And the old man says as he fixes his eye
And studies the whore from the shrine of love,
And sees the manner in which she walks,
And sees how she moves inside her robe:
'Woman of pleasure, woman of man,
Undo the belt, undo the robe.
Bare your breasts and drop your skirt
And turn a beast into a man.'

And she obeys by the water-hole,
And bares her breasts and drops her skirt;
And the lion and panther go their way,
And the deer trot by to drink their fill.
But Enkidu starts, and snuffs the air,
The air of Ishtar, the temple whore;
And his hands go out, his fingers search;
And she takes his hands and presses close
And guides him into the seat of love
While the animals drink at the water-hole.

Oh, wise old man, to have the art
To change a brute into a man;
To make a woman's supple hand
The fingers of a subtle mind!

The Teaching of Enkidu

For six days and for seven nights
Enkidu harries the seat of love;
For six days and for seven nights
The savage learns, the whore instructs;
Enjoying his eagerness,
Destroying his innocence,
Teaching him secrets
Unknown to beasts:
Until on the seventh morning,
Like a sower that has emptied his sack
And is tired of his long seeding
And longs for the water-pitcher and the reed-bed,
Enkidu withdraws from Ishtar's field
And takes the path to the water-hole.

But Ishtar's sweat runs down his skin
And human tricks run through his head:
The lion roars, the panther screams;
The nosing deer pick up the stench:
And when Enkidu bends to drink
Then every brute runs for its life;
Runs to the hills to lose his stink:
And when he stands with dripping lips
Calling: 'I follow!' all are flown;
So is his strength; his spunk is gone;
He cannot follow, for he cannot run.

The whore takes Enkidu by the hand
And leads him in tears from the water-hole,
He will never know innocence again,
He will never know his home again,
He will never know his breed again.
She leads him to the shepherd's house
And instead of grass, she gives him bread,
Instead of river water, a wine pitcher,
Milk from a bowl, not sucked from a teat.

She gives him a spear, to kill the wolf,
She gives him a sword, to kill the lynx,
She gives him a noose, to trap the deer,
She gives him a comb for his matted hair,
She gives him oil for his hard-tanned skin,
And she says: 'Clay of Aruru, Star of Heaven,
Now we must travel to Uruk, where
Gilgamesh, two parts divine and one part man,
Waits for your coming. Awaits
The coming of the Star of Heaven,
The Silver Clay of Aruru's fingers.'
So they cross the plains a hundred miles,
Leaving the Trapper and the Father;
The old man dozing in the shade,
The youngster pegging down his lines.

The Meeting of Gilgamesh and Enkidu

Near the gate of Uruk, Enkidu
Rubs the sweet oil into his skin
And combs his hair until
The ripples of the Corn Goddess
Run over his shoulders. And the whore
Takes off her robe, and ripping it
Down by the middle seam, divides it:
So, together, they enter the city gate,
Each in a half of the whole. And the whore
Slips back to the ziggurat, silently
Gliding over that timeworn threshold,
While the whole world runs out to see
Enkidu marching through the street.
And they exclaim with astonishment:
'But he is broader than Gilgamesh!'
'A shade shorter, but huskier!'
'Yes, his mother's milk was a lioness's!'

'But there is no telling him from Gilgamesh!
They are as like as two gods, two stars!'
'Which of them is the stronger, then?'
'Surely, this lion's son must conquer!'
Enkidu strides on until he comes to
The house of the bridal bed; here, he
Goes pale with rage to see the King,
See great Gilgamesh lolling at the gate,
Waiting to snatch the bride before the groom.
They run at one other like two bulls;
When they meet, Uruk's walls shake, all
The streets quiver underfoot; the posts of
The bridal gate shiver into sawdust.
They grapple; they sway; the whole city
Rocks with their wrestling, until they
Draw apart, to charge again.
But this time, Gilgamesh the King, the
All-Knowing Gilgamesh, thrusts one leg
Forward, planting the heel on the ground
And crooking the knee: when Enkidu is
Upon him, the King whips him over the
Crooked knee, and Enkidu is thrown, thrown
Stupendously at Gilgamesh's feet.
The rage gushes out of Enkidu like
Water from a fallen pitcher, and the King,
Laughing, pulls him to his feet, hugs him,
Cries: 'My friend! My boon! My Star of Heaven!'
To which Enkidu answers in an astonished voice:
'Oh, Gilgamesh, Gilgamesh! Where is there
Another such as you, where among all the world's
Wild oxen is there a strength like yours?'
So was the making of the love between
Enkidu and Gilgamesh the King.

The Armouring of the Heroes

Now, the King sets up Enkidu's couch
On the left hand of his own high bed.
The nobles of Uruk, the princes of the world,
Pass by the foot and kiss Enkidu's feet,
While the girls dance in the city and the bands play.
Enkidu chooses himself a ring,
And the dames of the palace
Pick him a wife from the finest,
And the happy King declares to him:
'Enkidu! My time has come
To do deeds that shall be cut in stone;
To write my name in those places
Where great men's names must be written;
To erect monuments in those places
Where none made monuments before.'
And the armourers of the city
Enter the royal room with forges and metals;
Under the eyes of Gilgamesh and Enkidu
They heat and hammer axe-blades
Heavy and rounded as the ridges of Hermon
And set on sinewy handles of box and sallow.
Scabbards of gold hold the swords
Whose pommels outweigh a bushel of grain;
Yet thirty times that weight is carried
By each when he is accoutred
With spear, bow, breastplate.

The Cedar Mountain

Now, they have left the shores of Euphrates,
With the people shouting: 'The Great Gods protect
    you!'
And after six days and seven nights they

Have crossed seven mountains and have
Come to the Gate of the Cedar Forest,
The Gate that swings on the perfect hinge,
The Gate that shuts in the perfect jamb.
But the Guardian of the Gate, Humbaba,
Whose ear can catch at thirty miles
Even the sigh of a strayed heifer,
Has heard them coming from the plain
And brought out his seven suits of armour,
And buckled on the first, and is buckling on
Six more, when the heroes shatter the Gate
And march on Humbaba's house, felling with their
   axes
The Great Cedar of Humbaba as they go.
And Humbaba screams in agony: 'My cedar! Who
   has
Felled my cedar?'; but the heroes only fell
Seven more; strip them; set them ablaze;
And before Humbaba is armoured in his seven full
   suits,
They fall on him; they cut him down with three
   sword blows:
His lips fly open with the smack of a parting kiss.
And the heroes stride on, while all the mountains
Of Lebanon and Hermon tremble for their Guardian:
And Gilgamesh fells all the Forest of Cedars,
And Enkidu tears up their roots: they hurl
The towering trunks into the streams
Which sweep them in spray and thunder
To the broad rivers of the plains. There,
They ride slowly to the city walls, and
The men of Uruk hurry out with saw and adze;
They shape the huge timbers, they section them,
Pin them; they make them into palace ceilings;
They frame them into towering gates.
Meanwhile, the two heroes have climbed
To the uttermost top of the highest peak, and
Staring up into the sky, they can see plainly

20

The Throne of Ishtar floating high above them,
And high above Ishtar the very palaces
Of the Great Gods themselves: the heroes know
They are higher now than any man before.

The King's Rejection of Ishtar

Now, Ishtar, looking down from her bed,
Sees Gilgamesh the King washing his long hair,
Rinsing his weapons, changing his bloody clothes
For royal robes, and putting on his crown. And
The Goddess of Love sings to Gilgamesh the King:
'Gilgamesh, Gilgamesh, golden king,
Throw back your hair and lift your head!
Look into Heaven and see the flesh
Of Ishtar the Queen in her royal bed!
A king to couple with the Queen of Love,
A king to seed a heavenly field,
A lusty king in a heavenly grove
Sheathing his sword in a queen's scabbard!
Oh, what can be richer than the reward
Of the king that sates the lust of a queen,
Who cools her flesh with a burning sword,
Who rides her belly like a ship of majesty,
Who paws her breasts like a lion in fury?
Oh, Gilgamesh, Gilgamesh, flesh to flesh
We shall clutch together, and you, my master,
Shall have chariots of lapis with golden wheels
Swept through the sky by sprites of the storm;
Thrones and thresholds shall kiss your heels,
Nor shall there be one earthly kingdom
Whose tribute shall not run like a river.
And for each seed you shall sow in me
One thousand more shall seed for thee:
Your corn shall hang its head

With a tasselled surfeit,
Your ewes and does drop triplets;
Your asses shall be big as mules,
Your horses shall run like flames,
Their manes ablaze like Ishtar's hair.'

When the King has heard this wooing,
He lays one hand on his hip, slaps the other
On his golden pommel, and answers Ishtar:
'Lady of Love, the rewards of love
Are given by the lover, to please the mistress.
Pray, tell me, Queen, are you in need
Of scent, of spices, of clothes to wear?
Have I any wine to fill your cup with?
Have I any food that would grace your table?
Was ever man born that could reward a goddess?
And tell me, queenly lady, why I have been told
That your love is like the brazier that glows in the cold,
That the door of your thighs open back into snowfields,
That the tower of your body falls on him that upholds
    it?
Tell me too why they say, in the vulgar way:
"Ishtar is like the pitch that smutches its bearer;
She is the water-skin that drips on the carrier;
She is the stone that falls from the wall on the stroller;
She is the broken sandal-strap that trips the wearer;
She is the spy in the city who admits the invader."
And what of those who have loved you, Madam?
    Was not
Tammuz the first of your lovers, and doesn't he
Now bathe the world with his eternal tears?
Where is the Man of the Birds, of brilliant colours?
Is he still a king, or does he now with shattered wing
Crouch in a dark grove, crying "Kappi, kappi!"
The lion you loved, you trapped in seven pits;
The stallion that rode you, you condemned to the
    whip:
You changed the adoring shepherd-boy into a wolf,

22

So that now he is hunted to death by his own hounds:
And I know too where your father's gardener,
   Ishullanu,
Is gone; he who brought you baskets of dates but
Ran away from your arms: you made him the blind
   mole
That is doomed to tunnel forever, always to desire
What he can never see; a creature of sighs.'

The Sending of the Bull

Jumping from her bed and flying upwards
In burning humiliation, spitting fire, Ishtar
Runs into the palace of her father, Anu,
And to him and to her mother, Antum,
Reports Gilgamesh's sneers. She cries:
'All my wickednesses, all my disgraces,
Gilgamesh has thrown them in my face!'
Anu says: 'Since they are yours and belong to you,
What better place?' But Ishtar answers furiously:
'He is swollen with pride! Fill him with more, Father!
Stuff him to bursting! When he can hold no more,
Send down the Bull of Heaven to crush his arrogance!'
Anu only shrugs his shoulders, so she screams:
'Refuse, Father, and I swear to plummet straight
To the Gate of Hell. I shall rip loose its catches,
Fling it wide open, and order out the dead.
And the dead shall spread their black wings
And swarm over the land like locusts, squeezing
Every living person off the face of the earth.'
Anu asks her: 'If I send down the Bull on purpose
To punish Gilgamesh, who will protect the innocent?'
Ishtar tells him: 'I have stored corn for the people.
I have hay for their cattle. They can survive
Seven years of drought, seven years without harvest.'
So Anu whistles on his thumb, and the byre

Of the Bull of Heaven flies open: looking up,
Shepherds see the flames of his nostrils, burning in the
  sky.

The Killing of the Bull

He drops – a speck, a spot, a blur,
Suddenly, a bull: at his first snort
Hundreds fall withered: his switching tail
Lays thousands on the sands: his eyes glower
As with his hooves he scrapes valleys
To divert the rivers,
With his horns tosses hills
To block the waters.
But Enkidu has sprung upon his back,
Gripping him by the horns, and Gilgamesh
Has raced up with his sword and sunk it
Between the horns and nape: in bursts
Of spume and blood, the Bull drops dead.

They chop out his heart,
Offer it up to Shamash:
They hack off his horns,
Hang them up in the city.
They hug each other, laugh;
All Euphrates sings,
Rings with rejoicings.
'Here's a deed never done,
A deed to cut in stone,'
Brags Gilgamesh. Then,
They hear an outcry
From the ziggurat,
Ishtar shrilling:
'The Bull of Heaven!
They have killed the Bull!'

24

And Enkidu guffaws: he
Hacks off the Bull's right thigh
And tosses it at Ishtar.
He shouts at her:
'So will I do to you
If I get my hands on you.'

The Judgment of the Gods

But while Gilgamesh is shouting:
'Who is the greatest of men?'
And every voice trumpeting:
'Gilgamesh! Greatest of men!'
The Great Gods are meeting:
Anu, God of the Heavens,
Enlil, God of the Earth,
Shamash, the Sun God. They
Speak shortly: says Anu:
'One of them must die.'
Enlil says: 'It shall be Enkidu.'
'What!' Shamash exclaims,
'The captain die for the general,
The lesser rogue for the greater?'
But Enlil says angrily:
'Who are you to talk?
Were the crimes not countenanced
With your bright connivance?
Did you cloud your face
When they slaughtered Humbaba?
Did you dazzle their eyes
When they sprang at the Bull?
Has his heart not been
Your reward for complicity?'
Shamash says no more, so
Mammetum, The Fatemaker,
Is summoned to the council chamber.

Enkidu's Sickness and His Dream

So, in the middle of the laughing,
The huzzaing and the singing,
With the flutes piping, the drums beating,
The people dancing, their feet springing,
Enkidu turns and says to the King:
'Did I turn pale when I struck Humbaba?
Did my legs turn to water when I rode the Bull?
Was I in a cold sweat when I wrestled with you?
If not, why are these suddenly my distresses?'
He goes to his couch and lies there
On the left hand of the King's bed;
The King sits beside him anxiously
Until Enkidu falls asleep. And the
Flutes and drums falter into silence,
Night wears on and morning advances:
Then Enkidu wakes up and tells Gilgamesh:
'I have seen a dream.'
'Tell me what you have seen,' says the King.

'I have seen a house under the world.
It is dark and immense. Inside it
Sit rank upon rank of heroes,
Princes, noblemen, and kings
With golden crowns at their elbows,
With black wings on their shoulders,
With shadows of servants at their feet.
On one and all, a black dust falls,
Falls forever and forever. Even
Archpriests of the holiest places sit
In those dusty rows; and from time to time,
A winged shadow rises, sighing,
To draw black water from a dark well,
To break bread that is only dirt,
To eat meat that is only clay. And
All the time, the black dust falls,
Falls on the servants and the kings,

Falls forever on the golden crowns.'
Gilgamesh says: 'What does this dream mean?'
Enkidu says: 'This dream is where I go.'

The Death of Enkidu

Six days and seven nights
The Star wanes, the King weeps.
As the term draws on, Enkidu
Looks back, sees in his mind's eye
That Star of Heaven, that innocent
Who lived with brutes, whose flanks
Rubbed theirs in passage to the water-hole.
He sees the little deer go nibbling by,
He hears the auroch's wheeze, the lynx's scream;
He spots the Trapper's eyes among the reeds,
Dodges the snares, detects the clever pits,
Re-lives the naturalness he shared with beasts.
'Til, suddenly recalling in his sighs
The whore that lured him from simplicity,
Shouting, he sits erect, and curses her:
'May your belly be glutted with men, and men with
    you!
May you be whipped from your shrine, to walk the
    streets!
May the gutter be your bed, the city wall your curtain!
May the good man spit on you and the drunkard
    thrash you!
You and your sisters after you, time everlasting!'
But Shamash overhears: he murmurs:
'Enkidu, Enkidu, this woman tore
Her robe in two, to cover you,
Accustomed you to bread and wine,
Led you to Gilgamesh, set your feet
On paths of heroic glory.' At which

27

Shame covers Enkidu; he calls back his curse
And sends into the air this prayer instead:
'Mistress that made me into a man!
May lords and princes love you forever!
May gold and cornelian enrich you forever!
May the faithful mother of seven children
Be left by her lord, in lust for you forever!
May the archpriest praise you to Heaven forever,
And lead you to the smiling Gods for rewards forever!
May old men's mutterings only cause you to smile,
As the young run to you, tearing their robes in desire!'

Then, the King touches Enkidu's eyelids,
But the hinges have snapped;
Puts his palm on Enkidu's heart,
But the drumbeat has stopped.
And the King howls and tears out his hair,
Thrashes about on the floor, beats the air.
His keening rings through Uruk,
Mingles with the dirge of wailing people;
And for six days and seven nights
Gilgamesh sits by his friend's body,
Letting no one lay a finger on it,
Refusing to believe that Enkidu
Is gone to the palace underground
Where black dust falls on golden crowns.
Until, on the seventh morning, the King sees
The Worm's head rising through Enkidu's skin,
And bearers carry the corpse away.

The Journey to Dilmun

Far away in Dilmun, the Garden of the Sun,
Lives Utnapishtim, known as 'Faraway': he,
As you well recall, was the one who when
The Flood came, built a great Ark in seven days

(Six decks below, but seven in all)
And saved in it one pair of
Every living thing. Of all men that ever lived,
Only to Utnapishtim and his wife is
Granted the Gods' reward of everlasting life.
So, it is to them that the King's mind turns now,
For life and death are always in his thoughts,
Plaguing him with questions, gnawing him; for,
Though he knows that Enkidu, that silver Star,
Has dropped into the underworld and sits in darkness,
And that the King himself must follow him –
The Star of Heaven and the All-Knowing King
Gathering the falling dust until the end of time –
His belly will not stomach such an end, nor
Will his heart rest until his mind has met
And challenged every argument. So it is,
That in his fear and in his loneliness,
And in his anger and his stubborness,
The King belts on his sword, and with a staff
Walks out towards the home of Faraway
To claim the secret of eternal life.

There are mountains to cross; the passes are cold;
The way is barred by guardians, the Scorpion-Men.
But when they see the King coming, these dyads
Know he is two parts God and only one part man,
And they raise the barriers, and let him through.
Four lions lie in ambush further on,
But his grief turns to fury when he sees them:
He hews them down with four strokes of his axe;
He skins them; he makes their pelts into a great
    garment,
And in this huge and shaggy dress, he pushes on
Into the tunnel that runs to the rising of the sun.

After one mile, the tunnel is dim;
After ten miles, it is utter darkness;
After twenty miles, it is dark as ever,

But the breath of the north wind can be felt
Playing on the face; and ten miles further on
The sun is rising and the dawn can be seen.
A last ten miles, and the tunnel is gone,
The sun stands at noon, and the Gardens of the Gods
Are blazing in full light: the trees and bushes
Hung with flowers and fruits of agate and pearl,
Cornelian, lapis, jasper, speckled bloodstone. And here
Is Ocean too, all blue and serene in the sunshine,
And near the shore of Ocean, the vineyard of Siduri,
The girl who presses the grapes in golden vats
And carries the wine to the Gods in a golden bowl.
Siduri is walking to the vineyard with a pitcher
When she sees the huge figure of the King approaching,
Hung over with matted pelts, sword and axe at his
    belt:
Running back to her door, she shoots the bolts, pulls
The bars across, and calls through the grille:
'Who are you, criminal, with your sword and axe,
All in lionskin, tight-lipped, gaunt, and sad?'
Immediately, he tells her where he is bound, and
    why, who
He is, and all the cruel misery of his story. Siduri
Listens to him patiently, and when he has finished
Pulls back the bolts, throws her door wide, and cries:
'Oh, Gilgamesh, Gilgamesh, All-Knowing King!
Are you All-Knowing, knowing nothing?
What is a belly for
But to fill with meat;
What is a gullet for
But to pour wine down;
For what a tongue
But to laugh and sing?
Feet and toes are for dancing,
Clothes are to wash in streams,
Wives are for men's arms to hold,
And little children born
To be led by the hand.'

30

But the King's face becomes sombre: he answers
    Siduri:
'Lady, I am in search of everlasting life. Where is the
    path
That leads to the house of Utnapishtim, the Faraway?'
Siduri points a finger at Ocean and answers:
'That is the path you want, King Gilgamesh.'
The ferryman is on the beach;
His boat is caulked with pitch
To repel the Waters of Death.
Steadily, easterly, he ferries Gilgamesh
To Dilmun, the Garden of the Sun;
Where the King, stepping ashore,
Sees to his amazement
That Utnapishtim, first of heroes, saviour of mankind,
Is doing no great deeds in his everlasting life
But is sitting quietly in the shade with his wife.

The Testing of Gilgamesh

As he did with Siduri, the King tells all his story,
Tears returning to his tired eyes when he describes
The happiness he knew with Enkidu. The hero of the
    Flood,
Who has all the time in the world but few visitors,
And likes nothing better than to tell those few
The full story of the Flood – how he was warned of it:
How he built the Ark; sent out the swallow and raven;
Beached at long last on Ararat – must now
Hear out another patiently: he replies finally:
'Two men, Gilgamesh, put their hands to a bond,
Does this bond hold good forever and ever?
Two brothers divide their father's estate,
Is it so divided forever and ever?
Yearly, the rivers come down in spate,

What they do early, do they do late?
While one sleeps, death takes another,
Which is the likeness of the other?
What is forever to the dragon-fly
But one day in the sun's glory?'
To which Gilgamesh retorts angrily:
'I had thought that Faraway, the saviour of mankind,
Would be making the most he could of his eternity;
Strapping on his axe, putting an edge to his sword,
Charting superb voyages: instead, I find
An ordinary person sunk in an ordinary life,
Preaching to me the ordinary sermon that
I have heard from every greybeard in Uruk. Was it
For this that I passed through the black tunnel,
Braved lions, blizzards, Ocean, and Scorpion-Men?
For this that I sat beside Enkidu's bed seven
Nights and six days, without ever sleeping,
Swearing to find the secret of eternal life?'
Faraway answers drily: 'The hero who can go
Seven nights and six days without sleeping
Has discovered already the art of eternal life.
Can you repeat the feat, or were you bragging?'
The King, taking up the challenge, says nothing,
But putting his chin in his hand and looking
Far past Utnapishtim, through the tall trees,
To where blue Ocean spreads under Shamash's eye,
Resolves that for six days and seven nights
He will stay awake, and win everlasting life.

The Proof of the Loaves

You know how, at the shearing,
As the fleeces are cut from the hide,
A mist, the powder of the down,
Rises unseen in the air and falls
Invisibly on the busy shearers,

Covering them with a white pall,
Much as the dust of the underworld
Covers the dead in a black cloak.
So sleep, too, falls on the eyelids,
A colourless dust, weighing them down,
Unknown, unseen, a weight of mist. So,
Thus, as the tired king, chin in hand,
Stares wideawake over blue Ocean, down
Drops the pall, and he falls fast asleep.
Faraway's wife says to her lord: 'Poor thing!
Wake him, now! Finish with his nonsense!'
But Faraway shakes his head. 'Wife,' he says,
You know what men are like as well as I.
Wake him now, and what will his first words be?
He'll say: "I haven't slept a wink." So,
Let him sleep on, but to teach him his lesson
Bake him a breakfast loaf each day at dawn,
Lay it beside his head; then, when he wakes,
He'll count his bread and know how long he slept.'
She agrees, and for the next six days and
Seven nights the royal hero sleeps; with every dawn,
The tally of the loaves tells off the days.
Until on the seventh morning, Utnapishtim
Wakes up the King, who, opening his eyes,
Declares at once: 'I haven't slept a wink.'
Utnapishtim answers: 'Count your bread.'

The loaf of the First Day
Is like a horse's hoof;
The loaf of the Second Day
Is like a leather boot.
That of the Third Day
Is dry through and through;
That of the Fourth Day
Moist only in the middle.
A green mould has touched
The loaf of the Fifth Day;
But that of the Sixth Day

Would bring health to the belly.
Now comes Faraway's wife
With the loaf of the Seventh,
All warm, delicious to smell.

And the King puts his head in his hands
And cries: 'Oh, Utnapishtim, all is lost!
Though only one part of me is man,
The hooded robber is beside my bed,
The Worm is waiting at my table!'
He starts for the ferry, but Faraway's wife,
All pity suddenly for his mortality, says:
'Give him a last chance! Tell him
The Gods' secret!' So, her husband calls:
'Gilgamesh! Can you find underwater
The thorny plant of everlasting youth?
It grows in the deepest water, it
Will tear your hands; but pull it up,
Carry it ashore, eat its flowers and
Youth will be yours forever and ever.'
The King shouts, and springs into the boat,
Lion-hearted after seven nights' sleeping,
And guides the boat towards the utmost depths.
He straps huge stones to his ankles and jumps in,
He drops like a lead to the water's floor, sees
The plant instantly; grips it: though its thorns
Gouge him like butchers' knives, he rips it up,
And powerful currents sweep him to the shore.

The Song of Everlasting Life

He lays the thorny bush upon the ground,
He marvels at the beauty of its flowers,
He cries for happiness, he dances round,
Washes his body with well-water, and while
Washing and dancing, sings this song of joy:

'Gilgamesh the King, the All-Knowing King,
Has sought and found life everlasting.
First of all heroes to obtain this flower,
Eternal youth shall testify his power.
Too late for Enkidu, but not too late
For Gilgamesh his friend. Oh, not too late
For Uruk's greybeards, each of whom shall eat
One priceless petal, and on bouncing feet,
With rosy, newborn chins, shall sing:
"Gilgamesh the King, All-Knowing,
Has fitted us again for dancing;
Has killed the robber in the night,
Stamped on the Worm, put out of sight
Terror of death and of the musty place
Where bread is clay, where the heroic race
And kings with crowns once bright as gold
Sit like black shadows; where the archpriest holds
No countenance nor seat; where every man
Sighs out Eternity – even the Star of Heaven.
Oh, Enkidu! For you and for your King
This happy song will ring on earth forever!" '

So sings the new-washed King, and while he sings,
A snake comes gliding quickly from the scrub,
Sniffs at the roses of the eternal shrub,
Gorges one bud, then, seizing on the plant,
Slithers away with it: when the King turns
To carry home his trophy, all he finds
Is a long brittle ribbon in the dust,
The hollow ribbon of the snake's old skin,
Sloughed when eternal youth came into him.

The moon waxes and wanes,
The fish swims to the hook,
The deer discovers the noose.
At the bend, the chariot
Turns, and disappears;
One day, the shepherd

Goes into the mountain.
One day, the King
Takes to his bed;
Empty sandals
Attest his feet.

Envoi

Uncertain Traveller, now you have seen
Gilgamesh's city, the city of Uruk,
Heard the story he brought back
From Dilmun, Garden of the Sun,
Read the tablets he engraved it on.
Now, walk this city wall again. Look
Inward again to Eanna's temple, to
The ziggurat where Ishtar raged when
The heroes killed the Bull of Heaven, where
Still stands the threshold so worn to the touch,
Where the whore still strolls in her old manner.
Then, look outwards again: see how the cornice
Shines like copper, on bricks baked in fire,
On foundations traced by the Seven Sages:
And say to yourself as you see these things:
'This was the city built by Gilgamesh the King;
He sought everlasting life; he died All-Knowing.'

THE PRETTY DRUM AND THE JOLLY DRUMSTICK

(A story of Sumer)

The Queen of Love
Found a willow sapling
Torn by the spate
Of great Euphrates.

The Queen of Love
Put it in her garden;
When it was grown,
She cut it down.

The Queen of Love
Made from willow-wood
A pretty drum,
A jolly drumstick.

The Queen of Love
Gave King Gilgamesh
The pretty drum,
The jolly drumstick.

The King struts about,
Struts about, beating
His pretty drum
With his jolly drumstick.

The girls of Uruk
Get angrier every day
With the pretty drum,
The jolly drumstick.

They steal them away,
Throw them into Hell—
The pretty drum,
The jolly drumstick.

Gilgamesh weeps,
Says he'll die without
His pretty drum,
His jolly drumstick.

Enkidu says to him:
'Don't fret, Gilgamesh!
I'll go to Hell and get
Your drum and drumstick.'

Kissing him, the King says:
'Promise me, Enkidu,
That if you go to Hell
You'll observe the rules.

'Don't walk in
Wearing your sandals;
You'll vex the dead
Who are all barefooted.

'Don't walk in
With a clean robe on;
Dress in Hell
Is dusty wings.

'Don't scent yourself
With oils and spices;
Hell's only smell
Is crumbled bones.

'Don't march in
Waving your javelin;
Many down there
Were sent by javelins.

'Don't stride to and fro
Swinging a staff;
They'll fly from crannies
In awful panic.

'Don't shout out
In a bass voice;
The shouts of the dead
Are croaks at most.

'If you meet there
The wife you loved,
Don't hug her to you,
She'll be a spectre.

'If you meet there
The wife you loathed,
Don't slap her face,
It is a wraith.

'Don't kiss the little son
You loved so dearly;
Don't shake your fist
At the son you hated.'

Enkidu promises:
He drops down to Hell
For the pretty drum,
The jolly drumstick.

Once at the gates
He forgets his vows,
Straps on sandals,
Dons his best;

Strides in scented,
Waving his javelin;
Swings his staff,
Talks in a bellow;

Sees his dear wife,
Wraps her in his arms;
Sees the vixen,
Clouts her hard;

Sets his dear son
Upon his knee,
Strikes at the son
That hated him.

There's a whir of wings,
There's a press of shades;
Enkidu is changed to
A void image.

Gilgamesh grumbles,
Waiting for Enkidu,
For his pretty drum,
His jolly drumstick.

He asks wise Enki:
'What should I do?'
'Pray to Utu
Is what you should do.'

He prays to Utu,
Lord of the Sun,
'Prithee, bore a hole,
See where they've gone.'

Utu bores a hole,
Enkidu floats up it,
Golden motes
In Utu's sunbeam.

'Good day, Enkidu,
May I ask where
Are my pretty drum,
My jolly drumstick?'

'The Queen of Hell
Enjoys them now,
Taps a web of dust
With a wand of shadow.'

FOUR POEMS OF MALTA

*

Winter Invitations to the Mediterranean

I

When the summer is over, they go home to the North
With their heads full of dreams and their eyes full of
    visions.
They dream of wine and pasta and red oleanders,
Their eyes recollect the light and the café tables,
The boats drawn up, the white reflections in the water.
When I write to them asking: 'Come and stay this
    winter,'
They reply at once like bereaved souls, full of longing,
Telling me passionately that they will come, of course,
December at the latest, that they can hardly wait.
And some of them even arrange dates, and trains, and
    planes,
Hardly admitting that these may have to be
    cancelled,
And I accommodate these hopes and expect my guests
And prepare their sunny room and order in more wine,
Until the New Year comes and goes, and silence sets in:
Their letters stop, or bring only news and affection;
And slowly I wake up from the dream and know that
    they
Have woken from it too – that the northern winter is
Their natural element: they can never leave it.

II

Why is it so for them, but not for me?
Why must they live winter, to love summer?
Why should drizzling days and running ditches

Bring reassurance of stability?
Must a man get up on sunless mornings,
Icicles in ranks outside his window,
To feel he's won by stern gelidity
His right to next July's spaghetti?
Why are a blue sky and green artichokes
Morally unfit in January?
Why February with no overcoat
Enfeebling to a Nordic probity?
Here, red clover blooms in March, with orchids
That make no claims upon propriety
But should remind me (if my friends are right)
That I am run to seed: spring will find me
Unwintered and debased, my backbone gone –
Flaccid, semitic, blowzy, and effete.

The Jewish Graveyard in Malta

Too few Jews here to justify a rabbi, so
When the double-door in the wall is unlocked
With a huge key and my friend carried in
– Dressed in a coffin heavily embossed with
The head of Christ crucified and bearing the legend:
I know that my Redeemer liveth
(How absurd, these religious confusions!) –
Three Jewish businessmen from Valletta who
Have never known one word of Hebrew, read
The service in English from a blue book,
Give the dead his ritual washing, do
Everything the Law has always prescribed.
Three smiling brothers in the Faith, correctly
Hatted, two in black felt, one in a white cap
Very like a doily. Oh, what a friendly way to be
Buried – and oh, what a friendly place
To be buried in! Orange marigolds warm

Under a blue February sky; white narcissi
In clumps beside the graves. Who are you,
Lucky people? I go to look, and read:
ELIHU SALVU, BORN AT LODZ, POLAND, 1842/
PILOT-OFFICER ABRAHAM SOLOMONS, KILLED
IN ACTION, 1942/JOHN MENDELSSON, 2nd.
LIEUTENANT, THE YORKSHIRE REGIMENT,
  MORTALLY
WOUNDED AT THE DARDANELLES/Here's COHEN
  of
LIVERPOOL/SIMONS of VIENNA/from the
BRITISH WEST INDIES, ABRAHAMS/ one ISAACS, a
VICTIM OF THE HUNGARIAN WAR. How far, how
Strangely you have all travelled! How happy I feel
To discover you here! The ground you are in is
Never cold, as LODZ was; the wind here is never
Sharp as it was in VIENNA. You are all returned to
The Middle Sea of your forefathers, the world of
Stone, dust, and olive. Welcome a thousand times!
                              Shalom! Shalom!

Maltese Goat

A goat can climb anything, but
What it likes best is a
Heap of rubble, stones of all
Sizes, unstable and sliding.
Each neat hoof-hold is
Only for an instant;

Somewhere near the top there's
A sizeable block
Steady enough to allow the
Long lunge forward of
The indiarubber neck, the
Straining upward of
The flexible lips,

The quick nip at the
Fig or the tussock,
The reflective chew in
A lightning zigzag,
The moment's dignity
In a proud eye,
The held poise, the
Taut silhouette.

Dear brother, they say you stink.
Well, so do I. Do you
Recognise me, aspiring one? I
Was born under your sign.

Christmas Oranges

(To Tommy Agius Ferrante)

Only ten days to Christmas
And the oranges are ready to pick
In the Boschetto Gardens. Golden
Globes in evergreen leaves, glowing
Down the valley in winter sunlight;
Every man running with his bag to buy,
Every stall displaying boxes and pyramids
Of golden oranges; and I, too, running
With my shopping bag to buy, to buy
My Christmas oranges – only ten days to go.
But my friend, who knows better ways of
Doing these things, gently stops me, saying:
'Never buy your Christmas oranges from
Those rogues, those sharks, those stall-holders;
Their price is tuppence over what is proper.
I shall speak to one of the Boschetto gardeners
Whose wife is the sister of a woman at Naxxar
Who is married to a man to whose uncle
I once did a most singular favour. This
Gardener knows only too well that his
Wife's sister's husband's uncle at Naxxar is
Under an obligation to me, and so he
Will supply you with oranges at a fair price.'
So, I have laid my shopping bag aside politely,
And though everyone else in Malta is hurrying
To the Boschetto Gardens, hurrying to buy golden
   oranges,
I am waiting patiently at home for the gardener to
Respond to the long-standing obligation incurred by
His wife's sister's husband's uncle, which is
Repayable to me in golden oranges, each
Cheaper, though only to me, by tuppence at least.
Now, it is eight days to Christmas; now it is
Six; now, we are seriously down to four, and I

Am beginning to wonder (not for the first time) whether
It is ever wise to accept the help of friends, whether
The dishonourable tuppences of sharks and rogues are
Not more provident in the end. Has the solemn
Obligation of the Naxxar uncle failed somehow to
Inspire the gardener? I only know that with
Only two days to go, all the gold has run out of the
    valley;
There are only evergreen leaves in the Boschetto
    Gardens.

FERTILITY RITES

What is this strange stone monolith –
Neolithic, holes bored in it, spirals
Adorning it? 'I'll answer for it,'
Says the professor of archaeology, 'that's
Fertility rites, that's what that is.'

What is this funny old archway – stone
Balls scattered at the base, a place
Where a pole went? 'Take it from me,'
Says the professor of archaeology, 'that
Was for fertility rites, that was.'

And so it is that everywhere we go –
Mesopotamia, Middlesex, Mongolia, deserts with
Painted caves – everybody agrees that
Whatever the site may be we can rest content
It was the shrine of those old fertility rites.

Looking backwards from nowadays – from these
Unsanctified times – I tip the hat I do not wear to
Forbears who went to such tremendous pains,
Backed up by their stupendous Janes,
To pay unwavering tribute to fertility.

46

How can we who never go to church – we
Who are quite without any type of rite –
Fail to admire forefathers who spent the
Bulk of their lives, the bulk of their dames,
In church, endlessly asserting their rites?

Those devout men had every chance – they were in
No way constrained – to do more field-work, to smash
More pots into sherds, to build stone bungalows.
But they scorned these material acts; they threw their
Whole being into church-going, to do their rites.

Darling, we are never told what they did – did
In church – we are not told. But you, darling, though
Comparatively slim, can guess, because you know
What rites like that are like. Yes, you and I have
Worked out together what rites like that were like.

Nothing worries me about those rites – those long
Prehistoric religious devotions – except a suspicion
That perhaps they never happened. Even granting
The zeal, the stamina, the crying need for fertility,
I am oppressed by an absence of hard evidence.

I think continually of the fertility – I mean
The fecund mentality – of professors of archaeology.
   The
Use of one all-embracing hypothesis is plain to see:
'Proffer me any site, I'll posit one rite.' Yet I, in my
   dubiety,
Ask still: were such our fathers, was such their piety?

THE GREAT LIBRARY

'Dig!' he ordered, and
They bent their backs;
Volunteers, eager to unearth
The Great Library of King Notheros.
After a fortnight, there projected
One chunk of snapped tablet
Visibly incised in cuneiformity;
Weeks later had emerged intact
One hundred; at last, ten thousand.
Lorries hurry the Great Library
To the crack museum; there,
A prof. with thick lenses and
Hairy ears deciphers; and after
Some years and all-too-many
Academic cat-fights, the world hears
[Five vols., largely footnotes]
What the tablets bear, what royal
Notheros carved with such care:

'I, John Smith, do hereby swear
That for twenty wackers I purchase
[Number indecipherable] amphoras
Of olive oil, the first pressing. . . .'
'I, Tim Brown, known as "Tiny", declare
(Witness these presents) that in leasing
From Arthur [surname defaced] the
Five-nublong demesne aforesaid. . . .'
'I, Jim, son of Wheeler, dealer
In leather harnesses, reins-maker,
Do swear [hiatus] pay not later. . . .'

No epics, no lyrics, it appears,
Were graven there: Notheros, it's clear,
Knew what life's really about:
Summum bonum, things that count.

KINGLAKE'S *EOTHEN*

Off Suez, Kinglake writes, a British gun-brig
Requested water, was refused; the hearty captain
Answered: 'Choose! My water, or your town!'
Promptly, they filled his casks; the Pasha was
Delighted to obey: not every day did power speak
So unambiguously. So, too, in Damascus, where
Our Consul-General, Mr. Farran, had run up
His flag: 'Let no Mussulman,' he said, 'deny
The European's right of way.' When one fool tried to,
Demetri, Kinglake's servant, horsewhipped him
Right in the public street; in consequence, won
Perfect admiration. So was it everywhere: no
Mule or ass for hire? Kinglake just took one, asking:
'How can a European travel otherwise?' These
   'Asiatics,'
He reminds us, need our reassurance more than
They need our money. Corrupt, misruled, and
Abject, they look to us to tip them off, to
Indicate the winning side: the captain's guns,
Demetri's horsewhip, bring happiness to men
Whose only aim in life is to anticipate who'll
Hold to-morrow's reins, to get a clear idea
Who's on the up-and-up; who's to pull in behind.

That was in 1832. Things are quite different now.
To flog an 'Asiatic' in his street has ceased
To be our habit or our ethic, would make us
Fear for our lives or blush for shame. And what of
Them, the 'Asiatics'? Have they changed too, and do
They blush for shame that once they kissed the whip
   that
Showed the ascendant power? I hope so most
Sincerely, but, I sometimes think I have my doubts.

HEPHAESTUS

When he saw them together, he slipped away
To his hammer and his anvil, and forged a net.
He threw it over them neatly, like a fowler,
And called up the Gods to see the comedy.

His wife became one lovely blush from forehead to
    toes.
Her lover's eyes looked daggers through the mesh.
The Gods laughed until their sides ached;
They showered Hephaestus with congratulations.

These ringing in his ears, he walks home.
The house is empty, the fire has gone out.
In silence, he goes upstairs to bed.

THE ELYSIANS

The town of Elysia is famous for its raspberries,
The raspberry-fields run to the horizon on every side:
Between each field lies a strip of water-meadow
On which sit huge white cows, munching.
The Elysians gather the raspberries and export them
In a traditional fibre box, to which is attached
An unbreakable jar of white Elysian cream.
Statesmen and heroes all over the world
Order Elysian raspberries and attendant cream;
Planes fly carrying them to perspicacious kings;
Eaten at breakfast, they show a star is at her zenith.

But the Elysians themselves never touch raspberries
    and cream;
They dote on sardines in olive oil in the summer
And on immense beefsteaks throughout the winter.

50

The Elysian men are proud, healthy, and sonorous,
With magenta fingertips from picking raspberries:
The Elysian women have fine rumps, and skins as
    sleek
As the olive oil that sheathes the sardine.
They also have ivory noses, and in each cheek
They display a flush that might compare to an apple
But is really the bloom of an underdone steak.
Oh, how I love to live with the Elysians!
To pick raspberries day after day with the singing men,
To milk white cows and churn white cream with the
    women;
And to go home to their stone cottages in the evening
And watch the sun go down behind the raspberry-fields.

TRANSLATIONS OF GIUSEPPE GIUSTI

THE POSTHUMOUS history of Giuseppe Giusti (1809–
1850) may be read clearly in the history of Italy itself.
When Giusti died, Italy was still neither a nation nor
a territory of one language; its linguistic divisions were
as marked as its regional divisions under a diversity of
rulers. Even its patriot poets, such as Giusti, could not
demonstrate that the word Italy denoted a particular
people or a defined nation: they were only determined
that a unity which had existed in the past must live
again. When Giusti pokes fun at himself in 'The Ball'
as the grumbler who

> ... *slavers and havers*
> *About Spirit, Art, History ...*
> *All those ancient cadavers*
> *Of glorious memory*

he is simply stating the arguments that were available
to the patriot who believed in the 'truth' of an Italian

nation: similarly, as a Tuscan, he is putting forward his own time-hallowed argot as the language of a united Italy when he speaks of himself as

> *. . . one grumbler who's*
> *Got it into his noddle,*
> *That for manners and grammar*
> *Home-chat is the model.*

When we read Trevelyan's *Garibaldi and The Making of Modern Italy*, we share the extraordinary excitement of those who believed that 'Spirit, Art, History' were grounds enough to justify the military creation of an Italian state. But we also recognise that Trevelyan's masterpiece is as much out of tune today as Giusti's poems have proved to be. When Trevelyan was writing, men who had fought with Garibaldi were still alive, and happy to press on the historian that glory which he was so eager to record. Much of the *Risorgimento*, then, remained alive until the first decade of this century – and Giusti, to the same degree, remained alive as one of its principal satirical poets.

Since then, the history of Italy has seemed to be a huge rebuke to the romantic enthusiasm that created it. There is no need to inform the informed reader of the multiple disappointments that have distressed the Italians of this century: it is enough to say that they have little emotion to spare on the 'glorious memory' of their grandfathers. What was demanded more than a century ago was obtained—to no glorious result. Today's Italian would not want to go back in time to the disunity of Giusti's day, but he might confirm despondently Shaw's famous dictum: 'There are two tragedies in life. One is not to get your heart's desire. The other is to get it.'

As poet of the nationalism that came before the nation itself and which was disgraced at last by Fascism, Giusti is a well-known name but a forgotten poet. One would not imagine there had been a time when students knew his poems by heart and a pirate press went to the trouble and expense of printing them in shabby, inaccurate, popular versions. The strongest evidence of Giusti's absence from Italy is the omnipresence of a single poem, 'Sant' Ambrogio', which the student of literature is still sure to have brought to his attention, at least at high-school level. He will be taught this one poem not because it is Giusti's best or most representative, but simply because it is the nearest Giusti ever came to the approved thinking of the present day. In it, the poet shows signs of recognising and even appreciating the unity of mankind, and the universal nature of pain and ignominy: for this short moment he adapts himself to an Italy that is still trying to forget the disastrous memories of the recent past. So, it has been Giusti's fate to be immortalised by the very poem that represents him least. Of this fate one may say, at best, that it is the sort of punishment which the satirist invites when he starts loving people instead of hating them: they are quick to take advantage.

GIUSTI'S DEMISE WAS CONFIRMED officially long ago by Croce, who dismissed him as a *'poeta prosaico'*. Professor Dino Provenzal, the editor of Giusti's collected poems, says that unfortunately Giusti himself confirmed this judgment. In 1844, he says, the poet wrote: 'A less agitated age is coming in now – half prose, half poetry.' This, until one verifies it, is an exciting statement, because it makes one suppose that Giusti had reached the interesting conclusion that political developments were making 'pure' poetry an impossibility, and a blend of semi-prose, semi-poetry, an essential form: Croce would then be reproaching the poet for dropping involuntarily a hybrid that he had conceived deliberately. In fact, none of this is to the point. Giusti's supposed agreement with Croce rests on a mis-reading of a minor poem. What the poet really said was something much *more* prosaic: in a little poem to a friend on his own thirty-fifth birthday, he confided that *he* was not feeling quite as agitated as he had been in his 'twenties and that he was going to spend half his time writing poetry and the other half writing prose. So we may say that once again the unfortunate satirist has had to assist in his own mis-representation. We may regret much more, however, that Croce's ruling has been accepted as authoritative by a majority of lesser professors, depriving Giusti finally of any claim to proper critical attention.

BUT THE MAIN OBSTACLE is Giusti's point of view, not Croce's. It is sure to startle us as much as it startles the democratic Italian, because it shows an attitude to personal and political liberty that we cannot share comfortably and must, instead, force ourselves to try and understand. Giusti has only one passion – the freeing of Italy from foreign rule, as the first step towards a new republic, 'one and indivisible'. He is a patriot, but not a liberal; he is a democrat, but not a humanitarian; he is an idealist, but not in respect to any country but Italy; he is a hater of despots, but not opposed to violence; he is usually an anti-clerical (though in the poem 'The Pope, Poor Chap!' he comes out in defence of Pio Nono), but always a devout theist. He does not appear ever to have set foot outside his own country, and he envisions the world north of the Alps as a sort of 'Gothic' landscape inhabited by corrupted 'Germans' and Slavs, all of whom regard Italy as a slop-bucket for their own degenerates or a mere field for domination. 'German and Grandduke' sums up exactly his loathing of Italian pro-consuls who worked hand-in-glove with 'German' overlords; 'The Snail,' which has a claim to be the best satirical poem ever written about the *bourgeoisie*, shows all his contempt of the Italian who made business-as-usual his way of life and refused to respond at all to the ideal of a free Italian republic.

In short, we must read Giusti as the spokesman of what today would be called an 'emergent nation' – odd as it may seem to regard the peninsula that has been our cultural cradle in the light of primitive nationalism. In this context, France is not seen as a sympathetic ally but as a source of corrupting affectation; England is not a benevolent asylum for the Italian refugee but the uncivilised creator of the gross steam-engine. Italian 'purity', unmarked by any alien influence, is always the ideal – and one of the curious and humorous features of this restricted nationalism (so at odds with the broader feelings of such as Mazzini and Garibaldi) is that Giusti phrases it repeatedly in *stomachic* terms. A 'Goth' or 'Russki' is one who eats and swills until he vomits; an Italian playboy or traitor is always a glutton for foreign dishes. Simplicity of taste in eating is shown only by the Lombard businessman, who eats nothing but 'the young growth' of the 'home country' – which is to say, destroys patriotism at its very source. It is touching, but not surprising, to find that the poet's last piece of verse, written on his death-bed, concludes with a menu.

GIUSTI LIKES GIVING the impression that he is only a common or garden democrat, not at home at all with grandees and 'Excellencies'. In fact, like many of the Italian patriots he came of a well-connected family: his grandfather had been Prime Minister to Grandduke Leopold of Tuscany and Privy Councillor to Marie-Louise, Queen of Etruria. His father enrolled him as a law-student at Pisa University, hoping he would make the law his career; instead, Giusti only benefited enormously from the fact that Pisa was a hotbed of 'unbuttoned' poetry, national rebelliousness, and satirical pamphleteering. The model father found to his grief that the son who graduated at last from Pisa did so as a happy wencher, an admired feuilletonist, and a green name in the black books of the police.

The glory of these accomplishments was dulled very soon by an astonishing misfortune. The young poet undertook the care of a dying uncle, from whose death-bed in Florence he was returning one night in an exhausted state when a hydrophobic alley-cat sprang out from the darkness and savaged him ferociously. At once, the poet's life became a fearful misery: he was unable to get over the rabid infection and, as Professor Provenzal neatly puts it: 'the physical infection put him into a constant state of black depression, which in turn helped to worsen the physical condition. . . .' Giusti found consolation in the affection of many fellow-patriots, including Manzoni and Grossi; but one may suppose that no consolation could make up for the fact that when Charles Albert of Savoy rallied his volunteers in Piedmont, the sick poet was rejected as unfit to fight. Elected a Deputy in the Provisional Government of Tuscany, he was quickly disappointed and enraged when a triumvirate of dictators emerged as the real bosses. Declining re-election, he retired to the palace of his friend, Gino Capponi, dying there suddenly at 41. His good-hearted father, who appears to have supported his son throughout his short life, supplied the stone monument on which Capponi inscribed 'the puff called an "epigraph" ' that the poet had considered suitable only for 'dwarfs'.

GIUSTI wrote a good many solemn love poems and many more topical, polemical poems of considerable length. But he is never more interesting and enjoyable than when he is using his great talent for pugnacious compression – reminding us, when he does so, that there is no fault more characteristic of satirists than that of over-cooking their victims. A dying fall (which Giusti dodges neatly in 'Mummy As Teacher' but does not evade so well in 'The Ball') occurs when hatred has run its course and has no more to say: in trying to say more, nonetheless, Giusti shares in the frailty, as he does in the vigour, of Swift and Aristophanes. But if, to boot, the reader finds him 'prosaic', then there is nothing to be done but put him back on the shelf and resume the processional Croce.

The Snail

(La Chioccola, 1842)

Here's a toast to the snail!
A health to a beast
That is brimming with merit
But extremely modest.
In matters architectural,
The spiral stair
Was inspired, certainly, by its shell;
While in matters astronomical,
To its horns we owe the telescope as well.
So, long live the snail!
A beneficial animal.

Content with the station
That God has put it in,
One could call it the Diogenes
Of the species.
It can take the air without
Crossing its threshold
And is so much at home in a shell
That it neither catches cold
Nor feels ever unwell.
So, long live the snail!
A proper Abigail.

When appetite languishes,
The bored belly craves
The savoury juices
Of outlandish dishes.
But the bonny snail
Sticks without fail
To the young growth
Of its home country,
Gnawing shoots, ruminatively.
So, long live the snail!
An abstemious animal.

Simple kindliness isn't
The way to success,
So we're forced to ape the lion,
Not the meek jackass.
But the snail has, inborn,
The urge to retract its horns;
Nettles, it never seizes;
It blows bubbles, and wheezes:
So, here's to the snail!
A pacifistical animal.

Nature, we know, is capable
Of every kind of miracle,
But (listen to this,
Executioners all!)
The snail is so favoured
That, on losing its head,
It grows a new one instead –
Yes, this sounds exaggerated,
But mustn't be deprecated;
So, long live the snail!
An example to us all.

Listen now, you homely owls,
Who pour stuffy maxims
Out of fatuous skulls;

Listen, Bohemian playboys and gourmands,
Drivelling masters, lickspittle servants:
Listen, I tell you, and with
One voice raise that chorus:
Long live the snail!
An example to all of us.

The Latest in Guillotines
(La Guigliottina A Vapore, 1833)

China's got a machine
That goes by steam
And works a guillotine.
If a thousand form line,
In three hours it lops
                    Their tops.

The puffer is such a wow
That the bonzes of the nation
Say China heads civilisation.
Westerners must now
Stop putting on dog
                    And stand agog.

The Emperor's full of probity,
Gruff, a bit stingy, on the dry side;
But he loves the commonalty
And he has sworn to provide
Scope for the inventor
                    Under his sceptre.

E.g., in a certain region
Folk were looking out of sorts
About taxes and duty on imports.
His Majesty sent them the invention,
And now you won't trace
                    A long face.

His work's so highly regarded
That the genius has been awarded
Sole patent rights in his engine.
In addition, he has been given
A pension: he's now a mandarin
                              In Pekin.

I heard a priest cry: 'What a wingding!
Let's get it – only needs christening.'
And I heard a howl from Tiberius
To his Premier: 'This is serious!
Why don't brains under *my* sway
                              Make headway?'

German and Grandduke

(Tedeschi E Granduca, 1850)

Once upon a time the word German
Didn't sound like the word Grandduke,
And when Grandduke was said by a Tuscan
He didn't think he was speaking German.

But the things that are German nowadays
Are so like a Grandduke's in their ways,
That German's good usage for Grandduke
And Grandduke's a German phrase.

So, it follows that the Grandduke's followers
(Those that follow the Germans, that is)
Must pay every respect to the German
Where the Grandduke's respect is germane.

Of the two, the German's the shorter,
Because the Grandduke stands on his shoulder,
And our money (to finish my sermon)
Supports both Grandduke and German.

60

The Pope, Poor Chap!

(Il Papa, Pover'omo, 1847)

Poor Captain Pope, poor Captain Pope!
Can't do everything, all in a twinkling;
Stuck on the poop without an inkling,
Most of the pep's gone out of the Pope.

He's only human and – same as a man –
Can't roll the world over onto its can;
Can't at once be a head that performs miracles;
Must first be a bum that hasn't barnacles.

Seas of debts on his quarter-deck,
The scuppers bunged with the century's goo,
Not enough cash to meet a cheque
And pirates abeam in a hungry slew
And asses and rogues to make his crew....

Goddammit! Even St Peter
Would have shipped water.

Sant' Ambrogio

(1846)

Yes, Excellency, I'm in your bad books
For letting off those little squibs of mine,
And from your eminence I'm sure it looks
Anti-German of me, to be rude about swine.
But do join me now in a little research
I made when idling round Milan t'other day
And chanced to step into St Ambrogio's church –
You know which I mean – the old one, across the way.

There was a youngster with me, the son of
That fellow with rather dangerous thoughts
Named Sandro: I refer to the one who
Wrote that little fiction about The Betrothed. . . .
Not heard of it? Didn't know it had been done?
Sorry to hear it, but I suppose that your head
Is so firmly bent upon matters political
That to switch it to fiction might prove fatal.

Anyway, in I go, and find soldiers there,
Hordes of 'em, from the North, no room anywhere:
The usual Bohemian and Croat soldiers
That are used as props in our vineyards here.
And how they did stand planted there!
In front of a general, you'd have thought they were:
With their tow moustaches and those mugs of theirs
And spines as stiff as wooden spears.

I pulled up short, because I was disturbed,
To tell the truth, to find myself pitched
Slap in the middle of that kind of herd –
(A feeling *you* don't have, Excellency: you're inured).
A stink hung round: there was such an atmosphere
That even (if your Excellency will excuse such words)
The candles of God's House on the great altar
Smouldered like tallow in the curdled air.

But, at the moment the priest took in hand
His consecrating of the Sacred Host,
Suddenly, from near the altar, a band
Struck up, captivating me with its notes.
Out of the mouths of the soldiers' band
A song came pouring, as from the throats
Of a people bent by hard suppression
And crying their loss of a dear possession.

It was one of Verdi's choruses:
Oh, how many hearts have known the bliss

62

Of hearing it raised to God by sad, parched
Lombard lips: *Oh, Lord! From our native hearths.*
And abruptly my old Adam started leaving me flat,
As if, by singing, these wooden boobies
Weren't boobies suddenly, but were in tune with me,
And me one of the gang, all of one family.

That's how things happen, Your Excellency:
Good music, written by one of us, well played –
In comes art and enforces harmony,
And out flies nonsense, bias, and rage.
But as soon as the sound stopped, my old devil
Crept in again slowly, and was gnawing my liver
When, like a trick, there came stealing
From those stolid dolls, like dormice breathing,

Slowly, slowly, a German song
Spreading its wings in the holy air;
A kind of prayer, like a lamentation,
So solemn, so plaintive, so sincere
That my heart still echoes its incantation;
And I marvel to think that such stiff dummies,
Such foreign blockheads, rigid and brainless,
Could voice so sweet a revelation.

I heard in their hymn the bitter-sweetness
Of the songs that are sung in infancy,
Taught to the heart at a loving knee
And recalled by the heart in misery.
Sad echoes of motherly tenderness,
Sad longings for love and amity:
Here was the cry of exiled man,
And my heart cried it back again.

It died away, but left me thinking
Stronger thoughts that yet were kinder:
What are these men, I stood reflecting,
But a king's slaves, banished here;

Underlings for suppressing underlings,
For smothering a Slav and Italian fear?
As sheep to winter pasture in the Maremma,
These are driven here, from Croatia and Bohemia.

Their life is hard, their discipline severe;
They are dumb, derided, and alone;
They are sharp rapacity's dull-ended spear
Pointed against others, not knowing it their own.
And the Lombard's hate of the German here
Keeps us apart from a communion:
Thus, we together bolster up a king
Who fears brothers, and reigns by dividing.

Poor fellows! Miles from where they belong.
Pitched into a world of hateful people,
Who knows but in their hearts they long
To send their lords and masters to the Devil?
I bet they howl, like us, the same damned song....
But, quick! Let me out! I'm growing so feeble,
I'll be kissing that sergeant, who, truncheon in hand,
Stands there stiff as a ladder, rampant in the land.

Mummy as Teacher

(La Mamma Educatrice, 1840)

Hooray for Adelaide,
Who makes my heart drum!
And from now to eternity,
Hooray for her Mum!

Wonderful woman!
Amazing being!
One in a million!
Really something!

64

Sunday, I met her
Walking the piazza,
Towing abaft her
Her growing daughter.

She swooped on me affably,
Opened fire sociably,
With: 'So delighted. . . .'
And: 'How goes it?'

And then to Adelaide,
Standing there speechless:
'Wake up, lackadaisical!
Why so feckless?

'Get with it, noddy;
Practice your duty . . . !'
Oh, lovable Mummy,
A proper beauty!

Then, grabbing my lapel
So I shouldn't skedaddle,
Cried: 'Oh, the years,
It's a dirty scandal!

'One minute you're green
And fresh as the grass,
Next minute, ancient and
Out on your arse.'

('Addie! Can't you see
I've not got all day . . . ?')
'My dear sir, won't you
Come out our way?

'Poor is our station,
Rich in *heart*, however. . . .
We count this an honour,
Even a favour. . . .'

('Oh, Addie, get cracking!
Don't stand like a stick!
Oh, Holy Virgin,
What a nitwit!')

'She's still green,' I said;
'It's to be expected;
She shouldn't be badgered,
Shouldn't be hectored.

'Age and practice
Will liven her stumps,
And with you to kibitz
She'll turn out trumps.'

At this panegyric
(Rare, I surmise),
A delicate smirk
Illumined the eyes

Of Mummy, who then,
Getting down to business,
Said: 'I see that you
Grasp what's in this.

'You know our home?
You'll come?' 'I'll come.'
And may I ask who
Would think I'd say no?

Came the day. I went.
Mum, from a casement,
Beamed on my advent
As beam the clement,

When a mumping friar
Trots up to implore 'em
To open the coffer
Maj. Dei gloriam.

With eyes glistening,
Both swooped to greet me,
Striking the ground floor
Like bolts of lightning:

Then, me in the rear,
Ascended the stair:
'*Watch* it, now!' they begged:
Watch the *legs*. . . !

'Seeing's not easy in
This murky light,
But man-traps larn you
How to look right!'

As we chatter our way,
Their teasing's fluent:
'Naughty boy!' they say;
And 'Little truant!'

Mummy, once there,
Hospitably bent,
Dusts the best chair,
Fly-whisks the saint:

With two quick tweaks
In a cupboard's bowels,
At speed unfurls
A pair of towels:

From a corner pitcher
Fills up a ewer:
What a motherly nature!
What a cleanly creature!

All her little tasks
At last complete:
'What on *earth*,' she asks
Is there to *eat*?

'Believe me, Addie,
I'm at my wit's end . . .';
Then (to yours truly)
Continued: 'Dear Friend!

'Hard coin in stacks is
A must to buy snacks with,
But my means to 'em wane
While my yen for 'em waxes.

'When I brood on this, I
Want to jump in the lake. . . .
Maybe *you*, lucky chappy,
Have got what it takes?'

Seeing her point in a flash,
I forked out sufficient cash
To assure Mum her ration
Of my compassion.

With a start of shock,
Almost of distaste,
Mum gave me a poke
In my bread-basket,

But nabbed the bawbees
('Just as a loan'): then,
Pursing her lips, she
Severely intoned:

'I'll only be shopping
A minute or two,
So you'll behave yourselves,
Won't you?'

To stop myself tittering,
I rose, gruffly twittering:
'Really, Madam, in all honesty,
Have some care for a man's modesty!'

Mummy bounced outside,
Clapped-to the door,
Didn't show her hide
For an hour and more;

And only at that,
With her usual tact;
Warning of her coming
With stomping and humming. . . .

Oh, Mummy, if you ever knew
What man would give for more like you!

The Ball

(Il Ballo, 1841)

Part I

Raddled *Chilosca*,
The Gothic beauty,
Has sent invites
To a swank party;

To an 'At Home' in
The mansion she rents
From Farinata's
Base descendants.

Magic lantern slides
Seem to play on the wall,
Painting goblins and fiends
Showing up for the ball.

In fantastic fresco,
See the antic dancer
Who skips to the tambour
Of the circus barker!

The horde swells, 'til
The court's a rout;
Hundreds, each out
To sport his snout:

Barons, Princes,
Dukes, Excellencies,
All bows and scrapes and
Reverences.

The flunkey's eyes
Assess each chest,
To what's pinned there
His yells attest.

Among so many handles
How ill-fitted *my* name!
How hard it jangles
On the ear – the same

As in a music
Solemn as can be,
When cornet or oboe
Is chirping off key.

With an Olympian
Nod of her crest,
The crusty, dumpy
Goddess of the feast

Becks and blesses
From her divan,
Into the mincer presses
Woman and man.

In clipped, laryngent
Vacuous accent,
Paid is the toll of
Compliment.

Off down the corridor
Squeeze the *bon ton*,
Buffeted, muttering:
'Pardon, pardon!'

Oh, hallowed rafters,
Portraits and busts!
Attuned to the argot
Of Tuscan dust;

If centuries of it
Fair gave you the pip,
May the pidgin of – *lodgers*
Come as a fillip!

Oh, stomach the breath
Of a rude villein,
Who has no more wit than
To talk Italian.

Backing and tacking,
Inching onwards *en bloc*,
Craning as from a crow's-nest
O'er chignons and curlilocks,

I reach a sort of room
Like a steaming copper,
Giving off a hum
Of rotting matter.

Here, seemingly moved
By occult forces,
A wooden congress
Creaks and prances.

German puppets
Togged-up in state,
Like birds wrapped
In a fowler's net:

Their leaps as stiff,
As taut, as harsh,
As spooks and skeletons
Dipped in starch.

No happy faces, no
Robustiousness;
Only a most elegant
Disgustedness.

Their spirits stoppered,
They open their pores
To the vapid thrills
Of tepid amours.

Their furred tongues
Of costive pride
Make endless blague,
But nought beside.

But of round and dance
They'll have no more:
It's a bore; and so,
To t'other floor

Ladies and gents all pour:
In furious disorder,
They swoop like rustlers
On vittles, bottles, butlers.

What barking and ordering!
What roaring and pouring!
What bending of elbows!
What shoving and clawing!

A vortex of swinjers,
Of snatching fingers;
Platters like mangers;
Titanic trenchers.

The belly's not asked
To stomach the lot of it,
Much of the spread goes
Home in the pocket;

And in the junket
Of joy unreserved,
A number of spoons
Creep off unobserved.

Part II

There, amid flaccid
Daughters-in-law, and
Amid their re-painted
Mothers-in-law;

'Midst diplomatists
In swallow-tails and braid,
As a-dangle with gewgaws
As a pedlars' parade,

I spot a posse
Of lower station,
Another specie,
Wholly plebeian.

Yes, I, who's guilty
Of a one-track fantasy,
Chasing like crazy
My love for democracy,

Am shaping a grin
At seeing such cullies
Picking their noses in
The Holy of Holies

And am heading their way
When I go all queasy,
Appalled to recognise
Four obscenities.

No. 1's the person of
A once-would-be friar,
Who now, for the hell of it,
Calls himself 'The Prior',

But has neither cassock
Nor clerical halter,
Bows more to the sauceboat
Than to the altar.

Beloved of the gourmand,
At grub, a dab hand,
He's feared but courted for
Cuisine of another brand.

He cooks-up the gossip,
He concocts the chitchat,
He decants the vices
Of this person and that.

He runs things down,
To pick 'em up cheap,
Then plays 'em up,
To sell at peak.

He's a hit at whist
With brides and daughters,
He makes monkeys of
Meddlesome mothers

And cuckolds of hubbies
Shrunk by years and paralysis;
Caught cheating, he chuckles
And bilks on his losses.

No. 2's blood turned blue
At his recent knighting
By a Christian King-of-kings,
By which I mean, ban-King.

He's bribed his way round
Both judge and priest,
Been set free to compound
Loans at high interest:

Now, scorning the pennies
Of the Florentine mob, he's
Got his screws on the thumbs
Of the proper nobs.

He flies his knight's banner
At their palace gates,
Enticing like a trapper
The insolvent inmates.

Like the putrescence
That slowly invests
The body in which it's
Become the guest,

But, sucking virility
From the host's debility,
Shares eventually the
Prey's infirmity;

Just so, the mouldy
Patrician – he,
Of ribs once peerless
But now shirtless –

Infects his eater
With his own hauteur,
Makes proud the creditor
By being his debtor.

And so, life returns to
Dead courts and palaces
As the knighted loan-shark's
Enfeoffed residences.

The illustrious ones
Detest him silently,
Pay homage and loathing
Simultaneously.

But he ignores equally
Hatred and dignity; he
Asks the kisses of the debtor
To play cat-and-mouse the better.

No. 3 will tell you he's
On the run – like a good book
Hot off the press, but one
That the printer never took

To attend the dinner
At which priest and censor
Chew-over what titbits
They'll cut out and devour.

Wounded at Rimini, he
Escaped capture and
Running for sanctuary
(Or so runs his *story*!)

Went homeless and hungry.
He says he dreams nightly
Of rope and drop: *I* fancy he
Sleeps like a top.

Oh, honourable sons
Of this our nation, sons
Of a century that
Decoys stupidity – oh, you

Magnanimous heroes,
Be alert for the cheat
Who feigns fear of the gallows
To elicit secrets.

Like classic Alcibiades
Of ever-changing norm,
This roving informer
Exists in proteform.

His disguise takes the style
That will be noticed least:
In London, he's an exile;
In Rome, a priest.

Among Royalists, he's a souse,
Raising his glass and crying:
'Friends! Here's a health to the King!'
But when he comes to *my* house,

It's *O Italia mia!* he
Croons with a sigh;
For the songs of the free
Make the tunes of the spy.

Part III

What horror struck at
Me, as I made inspection
of shameless *No. 4.* – that
Loathsome infection!

All powdered and painted
To pass for a chicken,
But toothless and two-faced,
'At Home' in the midden.

The modern way's to play
Awfully bored with dead
Titans, but for any Tom
Thumb of today, to go way

Overboard. From the riffraff,
You pick a palpable dwarf
And inflate on his behalf
A puff called 'an epigraph'.

So, who will suspect me
Of staging a farce,
If I choose *No. 4* to be
My horse's arse?

Donkey's years old,
Once rich, well-bred,
He got bored to death
By not being dead. So

He looked for distraction
In foreign lands; soon, he
Was top chameleon of
The pilgrim band. But he

Blued so much abroad that
When he had to come back,
All but his social rank
Had been lost up the crack,

And he must fawn for bread on
Peregrinating Russkis,
A shabby patrician in
Pursuit of gutses;

Guzzling goodies
From foreigners' hands,
To redeem a birthright
Eaten in foreign lands.

In threadbare clothes he
Struts and bustles,
Curvets and trips with
Jerky muscles, and

With the irony of
An elegant rudeness,
Piping in sentences
More French than indigenous,

Cries: 'Eh, bien, ninnies;
See how I run! How I
Make the grade with
Foreign chums! Who

Must first gorge their bellies,
So as to spew 'em empty, who
Boast like Hercules, while I
Milk 'em prudentially.

So, why the squawks from
Patriotic pikers? Nom de Dieu!
What's Italy, I ask you, Sir,
If she's not a taverna?

Do we want mine host to
Distinguish too nicely?
To ask well-heeled toss-pots
For their bona fides?

Better he learn that
What's known as 'honour'
Stretches every whichway,
In the manner of rubber.

The stodgy home-body
Who sends up such a groan,
Has a sort of home-sickness
In his bones. Why, I'm

Told of one grumbler who's
Got it into his noddle,
That for manners and grammar
Home-chat is the model.

He slavers and havers
About Spirit, Art, History. . . .
All those ancient cadavers
Of glorious memory.

But what validity
Has his currency?
I'm Royster-Doyster,
The world my oyster.

My creed's frankness and *élan*,
Plus always keeping going,
Stand-pats and thick-heads can
Have what's over.'

How was I supposed to
Rebut *No. 4*? Salutes of bad
Eggs is all I've had
When I've preached before.

So I hewed to *his* line and,
Though stung, said: 'How true!
What's Italy but a *rendezvous*
For pirate crews?

One does meet a few
Honest ones who
Come and go, with no
Axe to grind, no row to hoe;

For the rest, Italy's
A bucket; annually
It must catch what's vomited
From the Alps and the sea.

His cash buys each rover
The same obeisance, be
He bandit, slut, or de-
Bagged prince; and he

Perfectly naturally
Makes one of a *canaille*,
Punctilio not mattering
To the garbage fly.

Round this fair horde
With its shady cadres
Of self-styled Lords and
Their non-Ladies – round

This exotic jungle mess
Personified by human dress –
Presses the scum of our own nation
To dress the stage of degradation.

At the vandal wassails
Of Count Off and Count Iff,
We mete out the brio,
They fork out the *rosbiff*.'

'*Eh, bien*, your head wants
Looking at!' cried *No. 4* – that
Martyr to the starched cravat:
'Not only did I freely gather

Bias and gall from all your blather,
But *scruples* too! I do aver
You're no more than a greenhorn, Sir,
A babe newborn – *adieu, parbleu!*'

Off he goes, with the demeanour
Of a fellow who's in the know,
And who means to find more swallows
Before summer goes.

On the Death of Duke Francis IV of Modena

(Per La Morte del Duca Francesco IV de Modena, 1846)

At last, the ducal thug is dead!
God! Stage the march to his stone bed!
For his clergy – prison-guards, whom praying's left
   goose-necked;
For his last candle – at grave's head, a guillotine erected;
For his safe conduct – a passport, by Satan validated.
While blacklegs staunch their tears with office blotters
We'll crimp our mourning-bands – to frill pigs'
   trotters!*

––––––––––––––––

*Modena was (and still is) renowned for its pigs' trotters.

Two Epigrams

Whene'er Lucretia meets a handsome gent,
Love's power is too strong: she's soon recumbent.
Very few men are handsome, yet Lucretia
Seems to find every man a handsome creature.

*   *   *   *

Commonsense, once founder of a school of thought,
Is found no more where scholarship is taught.
It died when Science, its child, dissected it,
Curious to know what made the old man tick.